William T. George

BOX TURTLE AT LONG POND

pictures by Lindsay Barrett George

A TRUMPET CLUB SPECIAL EDITION

Published by
The Trumpet Club
1540 Broadway
New York, New York 10036

Gouache paints were used
for the full-color art.
The text type is ITC Bookman.

ISBN 0-440-84799-0

This edition published by ar-
rangement with Greenwillow
Books, a division of William
Morrow & Company, Inc.
Printed in the United
States of America
September 1992

10 9 8 7 6 5 4
UPR

FOR WILLIE

It is dawn at Long Pond. A white mist covers the water. Little warblers awaken and fly from the tall pine trees to the blueberry bushes below. They dart to the pond's edge and take long sips of water.

Something moves by a rotting birch log.
All the birds are still. The log itself seems
to come alive. The frightened songbirds
fly off to the tree tops. A head with red eyes
appears from within the crumbling tree. It is a
box turtle. He has burrowed into the log to
stay warm during the cold autumn night.

The turtle slowly makes his way down to the pond. He carefully stretches out his neck to drink. Box turtles cannot swim.

The turtle crawls to a favorite
spot where wild grapes grow.
He spends half the morning
looking for fallen grapes, but
finds only three. There is a
rustling in the leaves. The box
turtle looks around and
sees a chipmunk with a
big grape in its mouth.

The sun is high
overhead.
The morning chill
is gone.
The turtle looks for
a rock out in the
open fields, and
basks in the hot
sun. He closes his
eyes but is still
aware of the sounds
around him.

Gray clouds move in.
A breeze turns over the leaves
on the maple trees.
The box turtle opens his eyes.
He senses rain and heads uphill.
The turtle finds shelter under
an old apple tree. It rains most
of the afternoon.

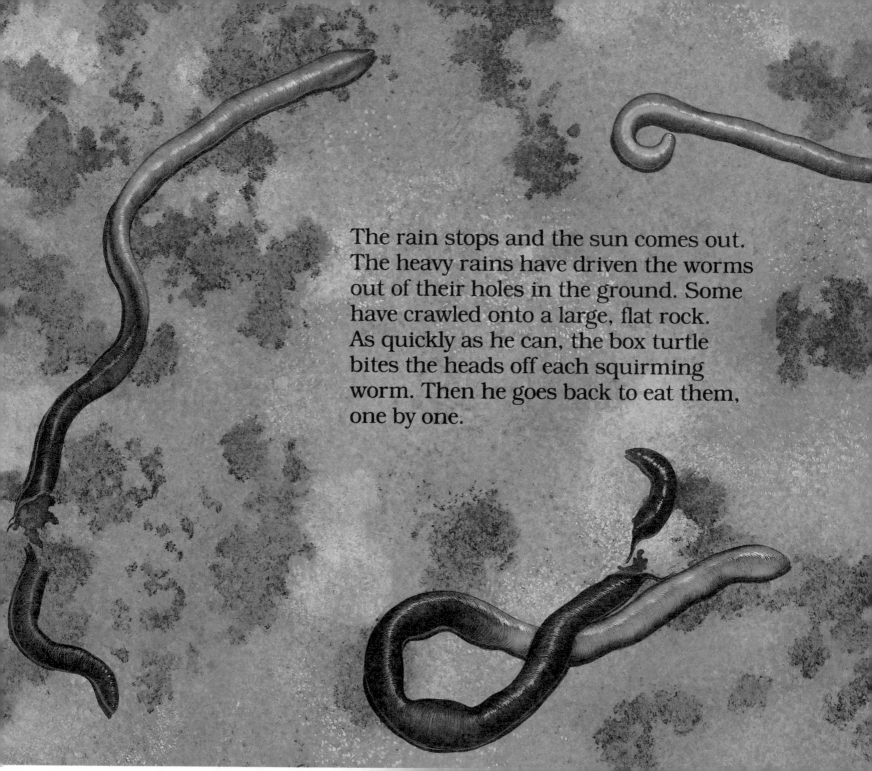

The rain stops and the sun comes out.
The heavy rains have driven the worms
out of their holes in the ground. Some
have crawled onto a large, flat rock.
As quickly as he can, the box turtle
bites the heads off each squirming
worm. Then he goes back to eat them,
one by one.

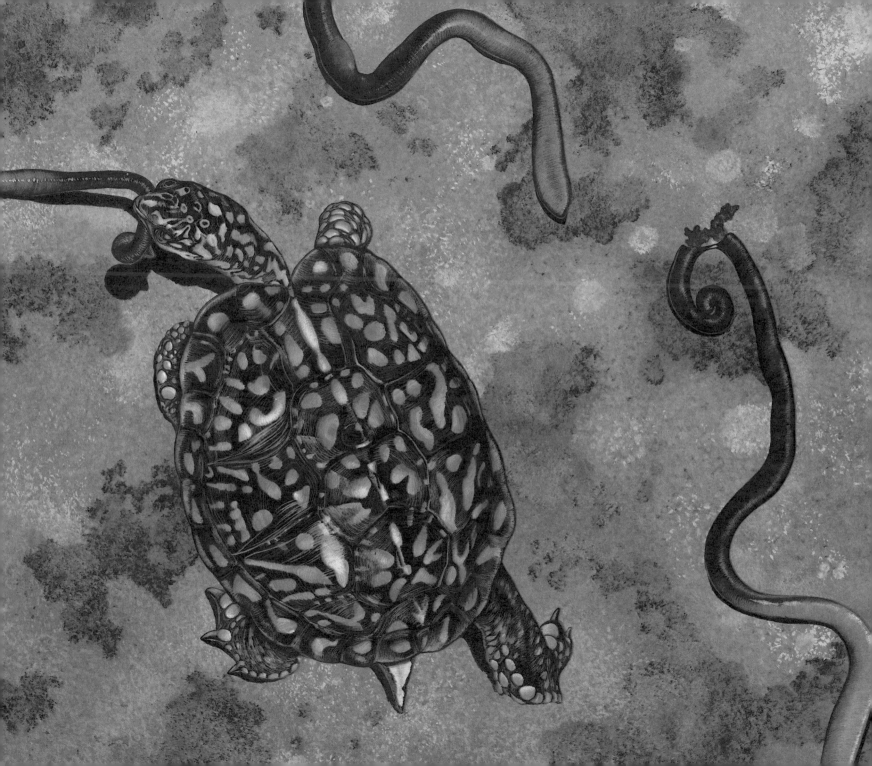

A young raccoon walks up to the stone. She is also looking for worms. The box turtle sees her and quickly draws himself up into his shell. The raccoon turns him over, but cannot pry the shell open with her little fingers. She eats the worms and wanders off.

The box turtle listens
and waits.
Hearing nothing, he
opens his eyes and then
sticks out his head.
The raccoon is gone!
He turns himself over—
the worms are gone, too!

The sun is dropping in
the sky. The air is getting
cooler. The turtle is still
hungry and crawls toward
the grapevines.
Suddenly he stops.
A grasshopper is perched
on a blade of grass.
The turtle opens his jaws
and lunges, but the
grasshopper jumps away.

When he reaches the vines, the box
turtle hears a thrashing sound.
A grouse is hitting the grapes with its
wings. The fruit is falling everywhere.
Another grouse is feeding on the
ground. He is frightened by the turtle
and flies away. The box turtle eats
grapes until he's full.

The sun sets on the far side of Long Pond.
The evening air grows colder. The box turtle
burrows in the soft pine needles to stay warm,
and closes his eyes. It has been a long day.